.

POSTCARDS FROM THE EDGY 2

A COLLECTION OF CREATIVE WORKS BY RESIDENTS OF MERCY HOUSING LAKEFRONT

EDITED BY:

Alyson Baron Woody

Ann Bihrle

James Conlon

Angela Davis

Laura Eberly

Jennifer Feuer-Crystal

Mónica Guzmán

Christine Makarewicz-Villaire

Felix Matlock

GRAPHIC DESIGN BY: Amanda McGovern

The concept, postcards from the edgy, was created by artist and writer, Ronald Routh.

PUBLISHED BY MERCY HOUSING LAKEFRONT © 2014
MERCY HOUSING LAKEFRONT
120 SOUTH LASALLE STREET
SUITE 1850
CHICAGO, IL 60603
WWW.MERCYHOUSING.ORG

mercyHOUSING

Live in Hope

The mission of Mercy Housing is to create stable, vibrant and healthy communities by developing, financing and operating affordable, program-enriched housing for families, seniors and people with special needs who lack the economic resources to access quality, safe housing opportunities.

Cover Art: A collaboration by children from the Austin community

Information on community history pages are from these sources:
Encyclopedia of Chicago
The Village of Grayslake
The City of Countryside
American FactFinder

Acknowledgements

Special thanks to all residents and staff that created and sent postcards for the book. Your art helped display the diversity of our communities and the many ways that the idea of community is understood and appreciated.

This book is dedicated to all past, current and aspiring artists and writers in the Mercy Housing Lakefront community. It is also dedicated to former staff person, poet, and founder of the Delmar Creative Writing Group, Steven Skovensky, who used creativity and humor every day to inspire positive change and help develop writers' artistic voices. And to our Art Therapist, Christine Makarewicz-Villaire, who for 14 years has created safe spaces with tenants to share, create, heal, and thrive.

Special thanks to the Mercy Housing Lakefront Board:
Lindsey Artola, Michael Borders, Michael Clune, Debra L. Grand, Fran Grossman, Charlie Hoch, Rhonda Hopps, Sister Margaret Johnson, Charles B. Lewis, Howard Natinsky, Jack E. Neal, John Neuberger, John K. Powell, Kurt Rogers, Greg Salah, Kay Whitlock

A special thanks to Sister Lillian Murphy for her passion, dedication, and leadership in creating healthy communities across the country as the CEO of Mercy Housing from 1987 to 2014.

Preface

We send postcards to family and friends to share the places we visit along a journey. The homeless travel many pathways of shelter uncertainty before they end up at Mercy Housing Lakefront. Other residents enter as children, finding affordable housing and services with us, while seniors join us at a different phase in their lives. The places each visit make an impression and are as varied as the residents themselves. Some have painful experiences from abusive homes, emergency rooms, mediocre schools, prisons, emergency shelters, and job loss. Others are simply in need of safe, affordable housing. All are welcome in the Mercy Housing Lakefront community.

The still popular travelogue for persons experiencing homelessness casts them as unfortunate victims deserving compassion from those more fortunate. Those of us who support and build housing for the homeless recognize the crucial importance of such mercy. The reality is the poor must travel farther to reach a threshold where threats of hunger and eviction become the exception and not the rule. But mercy relies upon the response of the subject. Oftentimes, the decisions we make, or those beyond our control, shape our destiny. Each Mercy Housing Lakefront resident has taken their own path to embrace activities that offer useful and affirming results. We offer help, but each person decides to take it and put it to good use or not.

Successful supportive housing enables residents to enjoy security of possession, respect for privacy and the reciprocity of community that accompanies what people everywhere regardless of social standing recognize as a good neighborhood. The residents of Mercy Housing Lakefront created these postcards to showcase their lives in a safe place as part of their journey. The diverse written text and images provide snapshots for the unfamiliar of the artful places under construction in the life of each resident. Security, privacy, and community at home in a supportive neighborhood allow residents practical freedom for self-discovery and expression.

The creative works collected in this book offer compelling messages and images worthy of public attention.

-Charlie Hoch, Mercy Housing Lakefront Board Member

Olivia M.

From the Editors,

Central to Mercy Housing's mission is the notion of community. Whether entering a new community, building new housing to enhance a community, or improving opportunities with people residing within a community, we are excited that Mercy Housing Lakefront has expanded its reach and community since Postcards from the Edgy's first edition. Our communities span from south suburban Illinois to the inner city of Chicago, up to Lake County, and neighborhoods in Milwaukee. Our growth provides us a richness in diversity and offers endless creative possibilities.

We loved working on this project with the residents of Mercy Housing Lakefront. Our communities are different geographically, but we have a common community of artists and writers who span all of our buildings. The poetry, postcards, reflections, paintings and photography on community are beautiful, unique, and tell the many stories of the artists.

Thank you to the children in Chicago, who inspire us and provide hopeful possibilities. Thank you to the women in Milwaukee for your resiliency and strength. Thank you to the seniors throughout all of our communities, who teach us with your experience. Thank you to all those that have left homelessness, for sharing your struggles, strength, and courage. Thank you to the artists for sharing your vision and beautifying our communities.

Thank you, readers, for joining our community.

The postcards scattered throughout the book are the works of tenants and staff at Mercy Housing Lakefront buildings that were then sent through the mail to other buildings. They used their creativity on the postcards to show what community means to them. By creating art and sending it, the participants increased communication among our buildings and shared their beautiful talents to brighten up the mail. The art helped display the diversity of our communities and the many ways that the idea of community is understood and appreciated. We thank everyone that contributed to making the postcards project happen.

PARADISE

Tile Drawings, By Ronald Routh

AUSTIN

Washington Courts Apartments

"What I like most about the garden is picking fresh fruits and vegetables. I like cleaning and helping to water the garden as well. I like seeing how the fruit grows from day to day. The garden plays a big part in keeping us healthy and active. During our gardening group, I learned how to plant things, when to pick them, and how to care for the plants during summer time. My favorite vegetable is carrots. I like the way they taste and they go good with ranch dressing! Before gardening I really didn't eat carrots a lot but now I love them! The strengths of my community is that I feel safe because I know everyone. Mercy Housing helps our community to better itself and takes the children out to fieldtrips also." -TC, age 9

"What I like most about the garden is watching the apples and cauliflower grow! This year we had big cauliflower plants that I helped water. I think the garden plays a role in our community by giving us healthy fruits and vegetables which make you grow strong. During our gardening group, I learned about what plants need to grow and what kind of strawberries there are. My favorite vegetables are collard greens. I like that I can pick them and my grandmother makes them for me. The strength of my community I feel is my grandmother. She helps keep me and my family safe while working at Mercy. Mercy allows us to sell the fruits and vegetables to the community, which makes me feel like a salesman." -JS, age 8

HISTORY:

The Austin community has gone through many changes, evolving from a bustling independent village to a dense urban neighborhood within Chicago. All the while, the neighborhood has retained its family character. Austin was established in 1865 as the seat of government for the Township of Cicero, a collection of townships in Cook County. In 1870, a town hall was built in Austin that still stands today as a reminder of the community's legacy. Austin began to dominate the neighboring towns, including Oak Park and Berwyn, and residents of those communities who resented Austin's influence petitioned for Austin to be incorporated into Chicago. Austinites opposed the plan, but in 1899 Austin was officially absorbed into the city. The community sought to maintain its identity, and though sweeping social and economic changes would affect Austin in the coming century, many residents would remain fiercely loyal to the community.

The 1960s and onward were difficult times for communities on Chicago's west side. The assassination of Martin Luther King, Jr. in 1968 sparked violent riots in Chicago and in cities throughout the nation. Austin was one of the communities hit hardest by the riots and many businesses and homes were left vandalized, looted, and burnt. Racial tensions remained high in the area and many longtime middle class families left for fear of violence. Neighborhoods in Chicago's west side suffered heavy population losses during these years, except for Austin which bucked this trend and continued to grow.

Austin today is a community of about 100,000 residents and is the largest community area in Chicago. Austin's tradition of family housing lives on with Mercy Housing Lakefront's family properties, including the Lavergne Courts, Parkside Terrace, Washington Park, and Whitmore Apartments.

Washington Courts Apartments 101 units of Affordable Family Housing est. 2006
Whitmore Apartments 54 units of Affordable Family Housing est. 2006
Parkside Terrace 62 units of Affordable Family Housing est. 2006
Lavergne Courts 158 units of Affordable Family Housing est. 2006

Gramma's House

I love going over to my gramma's house.

Even though one time I saw a mouse!

By After School Student, Age 6

Pigeons, By Anonymous

"You know, I try to focus on the good and not the ugly and the bad. I can see the bad that's going on in the neighborhood, but I choose to focus on me and not on them. I hold my head up high and try to keep a positive outlook. I feel that I carry it well."
-Dorothy Jones

Nature Nature

I think about the future, future.

Are you my destiny are you my beauty?

It's peaceful to me that I can see see
the Nature, Nature as the
future, future!

To me, to me

By After School Student, Age 9

Flowers, By Anonymous

10

COUNTRYSIDE

Countryside Senior Apartments

Amelia A. Kral is grateful that Mercy opened up their doors with affordable housing in this community. She was happy that Mercy Housing reached out to the community to house seniors who were struggling like herself to receive a decent and clean place to live that was affordable. Having the opportunity to move into this community helped her out of a deep depression. She had lost her senior apartment and was put on a waiting list immediately for a handicapped unit. When Amelia received the notification that there was a unit available for her, she felt that her life had been renewed. Having housing that was affordable gave her hope again and restored her faith in people. For Amelia, the strength of the community is many things: having neighbors who care, staff who support the needs of the resident, a property manager who cares, and a variety of activities that focus on self-esteem, health and wellness activities, communication, and respect. Amelia is not going anywhere because she truly loves living at Countryside Senior Apartments.

-Interview with Amelia A. Kral, Countryside Senior Apartments

HISTORY:

ountryside is a suburban community located 15 miles west of downtown
hicago. The land was originally occupied by the Potawatomi Native
mericans and later American pioneers. The first non-native people to
ettle in Countryside were Joseph Vial and his family in 1833. The
rea remained mostly empty farmland until the Great Chicago Fire of
871 when thousands of displaced city residents moved west into the
heap and open lands outside of Chicago.

ven with the influx of new residents, Countryside remained a quiet
arming community. This changed following the end of World War
I in 1945. The economic boom that occurred in the post-WWII era
mpowered many families to leave Chicago and build homes and raise
heir children outside of the city in communities like Countryside.
ajor housing developments throughout the 1950s transformed
ountryside from a farming town into a suburban community with workers
ommuting into Chicago. Countryside was officially incorporated as a
ity in 1960. The construction of the Stevenson Expressway in the
id-1960s brought further economic and residential growth to the city.
urrently Countryside is a city of nearly 6,000 and is home to Mercy
ousing Lakefront's Countryside Senior Apartments.

ountryside Senior Apartments 70 units of Senior Housing est. 2010

MY HOME

Geometric Shapes, By Michael Dixon

13

WHAT CAN AND DOES MAKE ME HAPPY IN LIFE

WHAT MAKES ME HAPPY IN LIFE IS TO SEE OTHER PEOPLE AROUND ME HAVING FUN. NOT JUST CERTAIN AGE GROUPS, BUT EVERYONE IN LIFE. MORE THAN ANYTHING, I'D REALLY LIKE TO SEE PEOPLE SMILE MORE OFTEN, NOT JUST ONCE IN A WHILE. IN LIFE, LAUGHTER IS WHAT I LIKE TO HEAR, MORE THAN ANY OTHER SOUND, NOT JUST HERE AND THERE, BUT ALL AROUND. I HOPE SOMEDAY TO SEE OTHER PEOPLE HELPING ONE ANOTHER, BECAUSE THEY REALLY CARE, AND ALL PEOPLE TREATED EQUALLY AND FAIRLY. I HOPE PEOPLE WILL LEARN TO ACCEPT OTHER PEOPLE AS THEY ARE. NOT EVERYONE IN LIFE CAN BE FAMOUS OR BE A MOVIE STAR. MOST IMPORTANT OF ALL, I'D LIKE TO SEE MORE PEOPLE LOVE THAN HATE. IT IS NOT TOO LATE TO CHANGE THIS. ALL THESE THINGS ARE THINGS IN LIFE THAT ARE VERY IMPORTANT TO ME, THINGS I'D LIKE TO SEE CHANGE. SOME DAY, WITH GOD'S HELP, THEY WILL.

By Patricia Lindstrum

BURDENS OF OTHERS

OF OTHER PEOPLE NEEDS, LET ME BE AWARE. LET ME GIVE WILLINGLY, KNOWING I DON'T HAVE A SPARE. LET ME NOT JUST CRY FOR A PERSON CLOSE BY WHO'S HURTING. PLEASE DON'T LET ME TURN THEM AWAY EMPTY-HANDED, WHEN I COULD HAVE SAID, "AT LEAST I DID TRY TO HELP," PUT A HEAVY BURDEN IN MY HEART, LORD, FOR TEENAGERS, THE HOMELESS AND LOST, UNSAVED SOULS. LET ME GIVE WHATEVER I HAVE TO HELP SOMEONE IN DESPAIR, NOT REALIZING WHAT IT MAY BOIL DOWN TO IN COST. I THANK YOU, LORD, FOR A ROOF OVER MY HEAD AND THE FACT I DON'T SLEEP IN THE DARK STREETS IN A CARDBOARD BOX I CALL MY BED! LET ME HELP SOMEONE, LORD GOD, BEFORE THEY DIE OF STARVATION AND HIT THE NEWSLINES ACROSS THE UNITED STATES, THAT THEY WERE DISCOVERED DEAD.

By Patricia Lindstrum

14

Snow Eagle Time, By Danny Beaird

15

Squirrel Brown Community, By Danny Beaird

16

ENGLEWOOD

Englewood Apartments

"It can be what it was before. Englewood was booming back in the day when I was growing up, it was even booming in the 1800s. It can reflourish and refurbish again. It can be redone to be back once again."-Irene, Englewood Apartments

HISTORY:

Englewood's history began in the 1850s as land that was mostly oak forests and swamps. The arrival of multiple intersecting railroads led to Englewood's original name, Junction Grove. In 1889, Junction Grove was annexed into Chicago, and at the suggestion of a city official, the area was given its current name of Englewood. Easy access by streetcars and elevated trains spurred Englewood's development so that by the 1920s the community had a population of over 86,000 with the second busiest shopping district in the city at Halsted and 63rd street.

In the years following World War II, Englewood began to see dramatic changes in the community. Nearly all of Englewood's White residents abandoned the community in reaction to Black migration that was occurring just to the east. Englewood's population went from being 98 percent White in 1940 to over 96 percent African-American by 1970. The dramatic shift led to enormous losses in population, quality housing, and civic services. While Englewood is still recovering from these losses, public investment is helping to revitalize the community.

In 2007, Kennedy-King College was relocated to Englewood's former shopping district at Halsted and 63rd street with brand new buildings and a 40-acre campus. Englewood today is a community of 30,000 and is home to Mercy Housing Lakefront's Englewood Apartments.

Englewood Apartments 99 units of Supportive Housing est. 2010

By Anonymous

By Anonymous

By Anonymous

By Anonymous

20

Communication 1, By Li

Communication 2, By Li

GRAYSLAKE

Lakefront Residences of Grayslake

23

HISTORY:

Grayslake is a suburban village located about 40 miles north of downtown Chicago. The area Grayslake occupies was originally home to Potawatomi Native Americans. The first non-native settlers arrived in the 1830s after the Potawatomi were removed from the land. Grayslake gained its name from one of the original settlers, William M. Gray, who occupied land on the southern shore of the lake. In 1880, the Wisconsin Central Railroad established a rail line from Fond du Lac, Wisconsin to Chicago which passed through Grayslake. In 1886, a station was built in Grayslake bringing economic activity and the beginnings of a downtown.

In 1895, the community was officially incorporated as the village of Grayslake. Shortly after, the arrival of a second rail line from the Chicago, Milwaukee, and St. Paul Railroad in 1895 further spurred growth and development.

By the mid 1920s, Grayslake was an established town with its own downtown featuring hotels, saloons, retail shops, and an opera house. The community continued to grow following the first and second World Wars. The largest spurt of growth came much later, though, in the 1990s.

Grayslake today is a community of 21,000 people and is home to Mercy Housing Lakefront's Lakefront Residences of Grayslake.

Lakefront Residences of Grayslake 70 units of Senior Housing est. 2012

24

"There's a saying where it says if one person goes for another, that's like one stick, it can be easily broke. But if you get a whole group of people, like a bunch of sticks, you can't be broken and you can accomplish anything that you set your mind onto just as long as you try. You can't just sit down and say oh that can't be done."
-A. J.

By Anonymous

By Anonymous

By Anonymous

"I've been involved in tenant leadership and I've been learning that it's not all about one person. It's about the whole neighborhood, working together."
-A. J.

By Anonymous

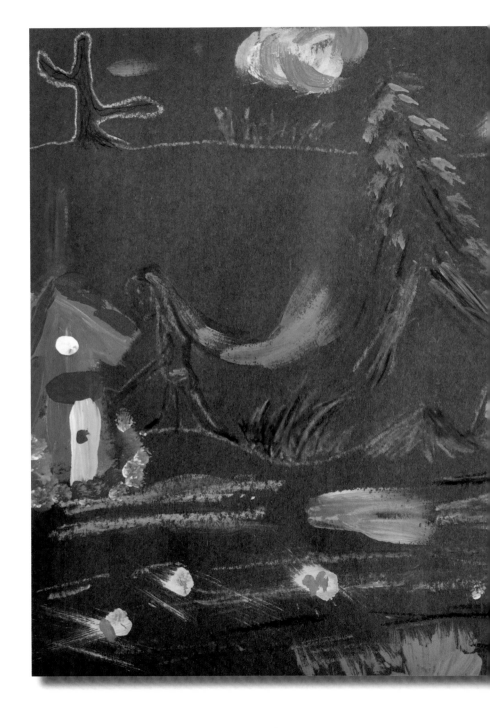

27

By Danny Beaird

28

LAKEVIEW

Belray Apartments

"I like the lake. It's our ocean. I'm happy seeing people enjoying themselves at the beach - there's no violence there. There's a poetic thing about the lake. Before a really big poetry performance, I go to where these jagged rocks used to be and read my poems to the lake. I watch the sun rise and then leave."

"It's okay to be yourself here. Sometimes I've lived in communities where we can't be ourselves - you have to put on a mask. I haven't had to put on a mask at the Belray."
-Gregory Pickett, Belray Apartments

HISTORY:

The Lakeview community area has many identities. This has historically been true from its emergence as a farming community, to its transformation into a resort destination, to incorporating as an independent city, to its eventual inclusion into the city of Chicago.

Once Lakeview was annexed into Chicago in 1889, the forces of urbanization took hold. New residents working at nearby factories moved into the community along with exciting new business ventures. Wrigley Field, home of the Chicago Cubs, opened in 1914 along with many retail and department stores.

The mid-twentieth century brought a boom of high-rises and multi-unit apartments into Lakeview along with a booming population. With the explosion of new residents and developments, long-time Lakeview residents began to center around their immediate neighborhoods to preserve what they felt was the character of their community. East Lakeview, New Town, Boystown, and Wrigleyville emerged as distinctive and well-known neighborhoods within the greater Lakeview community. Lakeview today has a population of over 94,000 and is home to Mercy Housing Lakefront's Belray Apartments.

Belray Apartments 70 units of Supportive Housing est. 1996

"Uptown" Northside, By 2166

If Only

If only I could say or see a star
eating at a restaurant.
If only I could see them making a
movie,
if only I could sit in the restaurant
and see them,
a star making a movie while I was
eating a meal.
They could pass by while eating a meal
and I would be seen also while eating
in a restaurant.
I would be seen on TV at the same time
a movie would be made.
What a day would be made.
Well I was just wondering.

By I. C. R.

Community Activist 3/28/13
By 2166

City Drawing on Canvas, By Kurt Rogers

What Is a Healthy Community for Kurt Rogers?

Loving your neighbors

Positive resources

Nice view of city

Safe community

Good schools for all ages

All ethnic backgrounds irregardless of race, creed, sexual orientation and income levels

These are the things that make a healthy community for Kurt Rogers!!

Community

The Community the
Community how great art thou.
I take a bow to the community.
How about the community
ain't it great. Walk around
and see how the community
can grow. But the community
is still growing. A community
needs to eat feed it fix it and
it will grow all around the
edges up high, and low, keep
fixing it (feel it so if can grow
big and strong and dress it
so it can see itself and say
I am rather quite, so it can
smile, and say someone
really cared, The community
smile and is relived from its
injure through the years.
So be of good cheer
and feed the community
and fix it so it can smile
again!

By I.C.R.
2013

By I.C.R.

"Neighborhood Nights is anothe.
project we work on in our
community. The main goal is
getting to know each other,
relaxing, socializing, and
having fun. We have games for
children to play, grownups can
laugh and talk, everyone can
enjoy the food that local
restaurants donate, and this w
we can get to know our next do
neighbors. I just enjoy
sitting out there with the
people. It's good to know our
neighbors because if a strange
came in, I might not even know
it's a stranger. It's good to
just be friendly and be around
people. Sometimes that's hard
people in supportive housing t
find that kind of community."
-Arletha Plair

By Ronald Ro

Haven

Many day the only thing
I want to do
In crawl into bed
And cover up my head.

Today, all I want to do
Is crawl into an iron maiden
And slam the door behind me

It's much kinder world
On the inside.

7/21/12

By Ronald Routh

Observation on i-Zombies

Every day I see people
Out walking (or driving)
Staring into an i-pod,
Totally oblivious of everything
Around them.

I once thought the i-pod
Was an extention of the person.

I now see the "person"
Is nearly an extention of the i-pod.

10/1/12

By Ronald Routh

34

MILWAUKEE

Johnston Center Residences

"My community here at the Johnston Center means that I will never have to experience homelessness again. I am safe and happy knowing that there are staff supporting my journey. I enjoy our neighborhood involvement both in and outside of the building with libraries, food pantries, and plenty of stores close by."
-Dorinda Sohrweide, Johnston Center Residences

Lincoln Village, Milwaukee

The Johnston Center Residences, 91 units of supportive housing, was completed in 2010 in an area on the south side of Milwaukee known as Lincoln Village. The neighborhood of Lincoln Village was originally settled in the late 19th century by predominately Polish immigrants. In 1880, there were about 30,000 Polish residents living in Lincoln Village who established a strong Polish culture which continues today. As Milwaukee grew, Lincoln Village grew with it. New residents who came mostly from the Mexican states of Jalisco and Michoacán, but also from countries in Central and South America, settled in Lincoln Village and blended their cultural heritage into the identity of the community. Today, Lincoln Village is home to a diverse community of residents, many specialty retail and dining establishments of both Mexican and Polish heritage, and two national historic landmarks – the beautiful Basilica of St. Josaphat and Forest Home Cemetery, final resting place of Milwaukee's famed elite.

East Side, Milwaukee

St. Catherine Residence and McAuley Apartments sit within Milwaukee's East Side neighborhood. The East Side neighborhood spans the area north of downtown Milwaukee from east of the Milwaukee River to the shores of Lake Michigan. Through the early 1900s the East Side was home to Milwaukee's more affluent residents, many of whom built extravagant homes on the bluffs along the lake. Polish immigrants settled in the surrounding area further inland, turning a piece of the neighborhood into an important hub for Polish culture. As the century progressed the neighborhood continued to evolve with increasing numbers of Italian immigrants settling in, reaching a peak in the 1950s. Later, in 1956, the University of Wisconsin-Milwaukee was established in the East Side neighborhood bringing in college students and young professionals. This eclectic mixture of people from diverse backgrounds gave the East Side its reputation as a center of multiculturalism. The spirit of the community continues on with the women and families who call Mercy Housing Lakefront's St. Catherine Residence and McAuley Apartments home.

Johnston Center Residences 91 units of Supportive Housing est. 2010
St. Catherine Residence 159 units of Supportive Housing est. 2013
McAuley Apartments 46 units of Affordable Family Housing est. 2013

By Ronald Routh

37

By CHICK-A-DEE

"We met with the farmers market coordinators [in Uptown]. We demonstrated to them how important LINK access is to the community by reaching out to LINK Card holders in Mercy Housing and throughout the community of Uptown. Finally, we convinced the hospital to apply for LINK access, and the LINK Card machine arrived for the 2012 season of the market. Hip hip hooray! We did it! Now everyone wants to celebrate LINK access at the Weiss market. The Lieutenant Governor Sheila Simon was at the market to tout the LINK Card access at the farmers market. ABC7 News was there to take video. A fellow tenant called me a celebrity but I said no, I'm just a concerned resident." -Jim Burman

38

Want / Got

They wanted white
    But got brown –
        They must accomedate.

They wanted him
    But got her –
        They must accomedate.

They wanted ~~catholic~~ catholic
    But got Jew –
        They must accomedate.

They wanted straight
    But got gay –
        They must accomedate

By Ronald Routh

2

They wanted rich
But got poor –
They throw the damned poor out.

In America
All are equal
Except the poor.
Money equals rights.

5/1/13

By Ronald Routh

40

41

Community, By Ira Brown

Margot and Harold Schiff Residences

"The Cabrini Green projects used to symbolize the entire neighborhood. Now, nothing is there to replace it. The people who remember how it used to be are left behind and have learned from experience that diversity seems to work better than just one type of group living in a neighborhood."
-Ernest Gladney, Margot and Harold Schiff Residences

HISTORY:

The Near North Side is bound by the Chicago River and Lake Michigan, which have both heavily influenced the community. In the mid-1850s, the original swampy marshes in this area were transformed into useable land for manufacturing and industry and a canal was dug through a bend in the North Branch of the river creating Goose Island.

A mix of working-class residents and manufacturing industries settled to the west along the river while affluent residents settled to the east by the lake. The Great Fire of Chicago in 1871 destroyed most of the Near North Side, but the area was rebuilt with the wealthy continuing to settle along the lakefront and the working class and industries roosting along the river.

In 1920, the creation of the Michigan Avenue bridge spurred the development of luxury shopping along North Michigan Avenue, today known as the Magnificent Mile. The decades following the Great Depression saw shifts in the community with the poor being pushed out farther northwest.

In the 1950s, land clearance and urban renewal allowed for the development of the Gold Coast, the neighborhood of luxury high-rises along Lake Shore Drive. By 1982, the Cabrini-Green homes were completed in the Near North Side, however, continually soaring land values and shifting public opinion toward the idea of mixed-income led to their eventual demolition in 2011.

Today the Near North Side is a dense community of over 80,000 people containing the Gold Coast, Old Town, Goose Island, River North, and Streeterville neighborhoods and is home to Mercy Housing Lakefront's Margot and Harold Schiff Residences.

Margot and Harold Schiff Residences 96 units of Supportive Housing est. 2007

By Ronald Routh

Community

Being a part of Uptown and mercy Lakefront

The church of God in christ is nearby
This Uptown place is a landmark; please stop by

Starbucks is within Target
They also sell clothes that fit

Giordano's has deep dish pizza to eat
Getting there is a Feat

Facilitators for Mercy's Lakefront; more than
just a roof) to live for us

They travel and spread their creativeness in
writing and Art groups in there own cars, not the bus

45

By CHICK-A-DEE

Community Poem

Knowing that God ordered my steps
before this world was formed. Why should
I worry. I'm destined to have wonderful
amazing things transpire in my Life.
I'm no longer fearful if I continue to
believe.
        In my life, I've lived, I've loved,
I've lost, I've missed, I've hurt, I've trusted,
I've made mistakes but most of all I've learned.
        Some people come into my world
as a blessing, others come as a lesson.
-By Von D.

By Anonymous

Lines and Circles, By Michael Dixon

47

Colored Lines, By Michael Dixon

48

PULLMAN

Pullman Wheelworks

"My community provides stability for young families as well as enrich life through education and employment. A place to call home while raising a family. I like the fact that it is on the south side, schools, shopping opportunities and places of employment; however it is plagued by violence and under-education and no socially enriching activities for the children of all ages. The Pullman community is a hidden gem on the south side of Chicago; it has walking and biking trails, and historical values that have not been recognized by Chicagoans. 'Evil prevails only when good people do nothing.' I believe this quote is relevant because positive change begins with each and every one of us."
-Candace Beverly and Family, Pullman Wheelworks

HISTORY:

The neighborhood of Pullman has a unique history among the Chicago community areas. Pullman was built as an independent town in the 1880s by railroad mogul George Pullman for his Pullman Palace Car Company, which manufactured railroad cars. George Pullman designed the community for his workers to live, work, and play all within the company town. It was originally deemed a success by many for its beautiful buildings and relatively clean environment, but troubles soon followed. Railroads were being built too quickly in the United States and the overproduction of railroads and railway cars led to a brief collapse of the industry. During this period, demand for Pullman railway cars slackened.

Workers who lived in Pullman housing earned less income at the factories, but the Pullman Company did not reduce their housing rents. Thousands of workers who felt exploited began to strike, which disrupted the nation's railway system. This lead many to question whether it was proper for the company to have control over so many aspects of its employees' lives.

George Pullman died in 1897 and shortly after the Illinois Supreme Court ordered the Pullman Company to relinquish control of housing in the neighborhood. By 1889, the town of Pullman became incorporated into the city of Chicago.

Throughout the 20th century, Pullman's fate was still closely linked with the Pullman Car Works. The Great Depression and the later decline of manufacturing in America hit Pullman hard. In the early 1980s, the Pullman Car Works closed its doors and its long history came to an end. By this time, residents looking to preserve quality of life in Pullman had already banded together to form the Pullman Civic Organization and succeeded at leveraging Pullman's history to have it designated as a National Historic Landmark.

Pullman today is a community of over 7,000 residents. The strong drive Pullman residents have to maintain their community and preserve its unique history lives on with Mercy Housing Lakefront's Pullman Wheelworks Apartments, a former railcar manufacturing facility turned family housing complex.

Pullman Wheelworks 210 units of Affordable Family Housing est. 2012

By Michael Carroll

51

By Brenda Twine

By Ronald Routh

"No friends, just associates. But I accept that everybody is different. God didn't make nobody the same. I mean, we've got the same nose and mouth and we've got two arms and two legs, but we're different. God made everybody a little bit different, but he got us formed up right. I respect my neighbors, they are as human as everybody."
-Ronnie Mitchell

Walls

The Chinese built a wall
 To keep out the hated Mongols.
The Romans built a wall
 To keep out the hated Scots.
The French built a wall
 To keep out the hated Germans,
The Americans built a wall
 To keep out the hated Mexicans.
The Israels are building a wall
 To keep the hated Palestinians
 Off their own land.
I've built a wall
 Around my mind
 To keep out the haters.

All the walls are the same,
They're all failures.
12/13/13

By Ronald

By Anita Alexander

By Ronald Routh

"I just love the neighborhood. It's not all one color, it's a diverse
background and I've got the stores right in the neighborhood. I've go
anything, I've got restaurants right here in the neighborhood. And yo
can go three blocks up or three blocks over and you never meet the
same people twice, you know? It's diverse backgrounds. That's why I
like it."
-A. J.

By Anne Heathcock

ROSELAND

Wentworth Commons

HISTORY:

Roseland began in the 1840s as a small Dutch farming village between what is now 103rd and 111th streets, gaining its name from the beautiful flowers which filled the neighborhood. Fortunes changed for Roseland when railroad tycoon George M. Pullman built his industrial city to manufacture his famous "Palace" railway coaches between Roseland and Lake Calumet to the east. Immigrants and skilled laborers from all over Europe came to work in the Pullman factories and many settled in Roseland.

By the time Roseland was incorporated into Chicago in 1892, it had transformed from a small farming town into an ethnically diverse social and commercial hub. The population grew and business flourished along Michigan Avenue serving all of Chicago's south side. The prosperity did not last, unfortunately. In the 1960s when Chicago's famous steel mills began to close, the Pullman factories scaled back production. By 1981, the Pullman factories closed completely and the neighborhood's main source of jobs was forever lost.

The rapid transition was hard for Roseland. Crime, violence, and urban decay followed forcing many longtime residents to leave the community. Roseland is still recovering from the losses it experienced, but neighborhood and community organizations are working to restore the area.

Roseland today is a community of about 44,000 and is home to Mercy Housing Lakefront's Wentworth Commons, Holland Apartments, Roseland Place and Roseland Village Grand Families Apartments.

Holland Apartments 81 units of Supportive Housing for Individuals and Families est. 2001
Wentworth Commons 51 units of Supportive Housing for Individuals and Families est. 2005
Roseland Place Apartments 60 units of Senior Housing est. 2011
Roseland Village Grand Families Apartments 10 units of Multifamily Housing est. 2012

By Albert Reed

By Albert Reed

60

Sisterhood, By Li

Community to me is:

1. Saying hello to a stranger.
2. Helping a neighbor with their groceries/no charge
3. Smiling at someone as you pass them by.
4. Helping a Senior/disable across the Street.
5. Getting to know your neighbor.
6. Invite a Neighbor to Church.
7. Pitching your trash in the proper place.
8. Talking politely to each other.
9. Respect one another.
10. Sharing helpful information.
11. Taking time out to Listen.
12. Recycling.
13. Being mindful.
14. Reporting Crime in the Community.
15. keeping our parks Safe and Clean.
16. Compliment Someone.
17. Volunteering if you can.

Ollie Mason

By Ollie Mason

"A person that hides behind a wall, you don't get to know them. You might speak some other language, but when it comes down to it all, we want safety. We want to be able to go out to the store any time of night and stay safe. They want their kids to be able to go to the playground and play without getting attacked. They want, we want, that's what we all want."
-A. J.

"Community work and Tenant Leadership [a Resident Services project of Mercy Housing Lakefront] are all about helping people to see how their needs are connected to the needs of others and how we can work together to make changes and get those needs met."
-Arletha Plair

By Ronald Routh

"It has changed here [in Uptown] since the early nineties. More homelessness. Mainly just the homelessness. It's more expensive, far more expensive now. And with those condos coming up and with changing those apartments into condos, it's going to be more expensive. And where are those people going?"
-Deborah Watson

By Ronald Routh

"Did you see that?"

"Can you smell that?"

"What is that?"

That is Uptown...

"Which way do I go?"

What do I want to know...

"Man!   That bus is running slow."

That is Uptown...

"Who do I need to see?"

Boy! I sho wish that was me."

"Is it this or is it that street?"

That is Uptown....

"What are they giving away?"

I dont want to go.   I really want to stay.

Each dancer to the piper must pay,

Everyday in Uptown.

What's the coolest part of town?
Where people from all walks of life can be found...

...And everybody has a friend somewhere around.

That is Uptown...

An atmosphere of joy & pain,
Many lifestyles of loss & gain,
Why can't all things stay the same...
Why does our neighborhood have to change...

Where is Uptown?

What is Uptown?

That is Uptown...

By P. Harkim

SOUTH LOOP

South Loop Apartments

The South Loop is a dynamic residential community just south of the Loop. Manufacturing, lumber, and commercial industries were initially drawn to the area due to the many railroads which ran through the community.

By 1853, the South Loop was officially incorporated into the city of Chicago. It's proximity to downtown attracted many of Chicago's elite who built large, beautiful mansions along its streets -most notably along Prairie Avenue.

In 1871, the Great Chicago Fire burned the city to the north but spared the South Loop. Businesses and industries displaced by the Great Fire began to establish themselves in the South Loop driving out many of the wealthy families. The South Loop soon gained a reputation for being a vice district known for its warehouses, brothels, and gambling dens. The character of the neighborhood changed again when in the 1920s the famous museums of Chicago were built along the South Loop's lakefront, including the Field Museum and Adler Planetarium. In the 1960s, families began to return to the South Loop and land previously used for manufacturing and railroads were converted to housing developments.

Currently, about 21,000 people live in the highrises and townhomes which pervade the formerly industrial community, including Mercy Housing Lakefront's South Loop Apartments.

South Loop Apartments 207 units of Supportive Housing est. 2000

A Lot To See, By Jeffrey L. Bradley

BY: Kevin Ellis

Time and Time again I've asked myself what's my Purpose in life? Being homeless is such a uphill climb that its easy to lose Sight. Am I living my life or Am I Just EXSisting. I feel obtaining housing here at the Johnston Center has given me the opportunity to live my life with positive Support. There is so much more to being homeless than Just housing. I feel we as a Community can take are former Experience's and transform them into tools to move forward with are lives.

For Every broken thing thats mended A Stronger vessel Stands in place holding more. Standing **Firmer**, Enduring longer. The true beauty is its uniqueness no two can be broken alike. we all have had are lives broken in pieces but now we Stand Firm mended back Together.

By Kevin Ellis

68

By Jeffrey L. Bradley

By Jeffrey L. Bradley

70

UPTOWN

Harold Washington Apartments

"When I think of Uptown, I see myself riding my bike toward the lake while gazing at the beauty of the city. Uptown has given me the opportunity to experience cultural diversity and learn to allow people back in my space." -Deidrea M. Zellers, Miriam Apartments

Uptown's rich history began in the late 1870s with a mix of multifamily housing and lakefront mansions. In the early decades of the 1900s, Uptown styled itself as a glamorous district with famous department stores and grand theaters, including the Uptown Theater, the Riviera, and the Aragon Ballroom.

Circumstances changed during the Great Depression and World War II when a national housing crisis and wave of migrants caused landlords to convert luxury apartments into smaller accommodations and brought in a new mix of residents. In the 1960s, land clearance and urban renewal threatened to displace hundreds in Uptown, but residents banded together in community organizations to preserve housing, improve conditions, and keep the community affordable. Lakefront SRO Corporation, now Mercy Housing Lakefront, was one of the many social service agencies which opened to serve the needs of Uptown's community.

Uptown today boasts a diverse population of over 56,000 and is home to seven Mercy Housing Lakefront properties including the Carlton Terrace, Delmar, Harold Washington, Malden Arms, Miriam, Major Jenkins, and 850 Eastwood.

Harold Washington Apartments 69 units of Supportive Housing est. 1989
Malden Arms Apartments 83 units of Supportive Housing est. 1991
Miriam Apartments 66 units of Supportive Housing est. 1992
Carlton Terrace Apartments 70 units of Supportive Housing est. 1993
Delmar Apartments 163 units of Supportive Housing est. 1994
Major Jenkins 160 units of Supportive Housing est. 1995
850 Eastwood 231 units of Multifamily Housing est. 2009

By Jeffrey L. Bradley

"I like Uptown a lot. I'm friendly. I like to talk. And, that's something that I had to learn, how to talk to people. You know, how to share myself with people and get people to share themselves with me."
-Deborah Watson

HAIKU FOR ST CATHERINE RESIDENCE

Tiny newborn child

On crowded elevator

Grumpy women smile

By M. Kastner

DDL Creations, By Anonymous

By Steven L. Kelley

Silent Voices

Silent voices crying in the night.
Lost souls crying for help, but no one
hears.

Lost children sick in the madness are
overlooked. Soldiers coming home
from war only to find out they have
no home or voice to be heard.

Homeless people looking for a park or
corner to sleep in for the night.
But all they get is, "Move on. You ca
sleep here."

Faceless people asking for money at
the corner. I just want something to
eat and you walk by.

Only when someone is put in the
hospital then you say something has t
be done with "those people." We can'
have them around our condos and our
nine cars.

Besides we don't want to see them on
our streets. Just make them go away.
That way we will feel better about
ourselves.

Besides it is not my problem.

By A. J.

Community Ditty by Apic

My community
Is a great place to be
Laughter feels the air
People don't have a care
I never feel alone
And now I'm not unknown

You Got to smell The Roses by Apic

There's so much pleasure In the world
That's close enough to touch
But we're very busy with many things
We overlook so much

There's so much beauty we can see
And pleasant sounds to hear
I love living in my community
With neighbors and friends so near

So, as the flowers of life
Pass by our noses
Don't forget to take some time
To stop and smell the roses

By Apic

76

"Artists in Bloom"
One of the beauties of community living is when we can come together expressing our
individual creativity and produce a piece of art that reflects the environment we
desire; colorful, vibrant & lively. The art pieces now hang in the Community Dining
Room, at St Catherine Residence for all to see and enjoy. Mrs. Jean Brite, curator;
the residents of St. Catherine's would like to thank you, for your support and
efforts of making the art classes possible.

By Paula Williams

A collaboration by Women from St. Catherine Residence

SEARCH FOR TRANQUILITY

Dorian Morningstar

By Dorian Morningstar

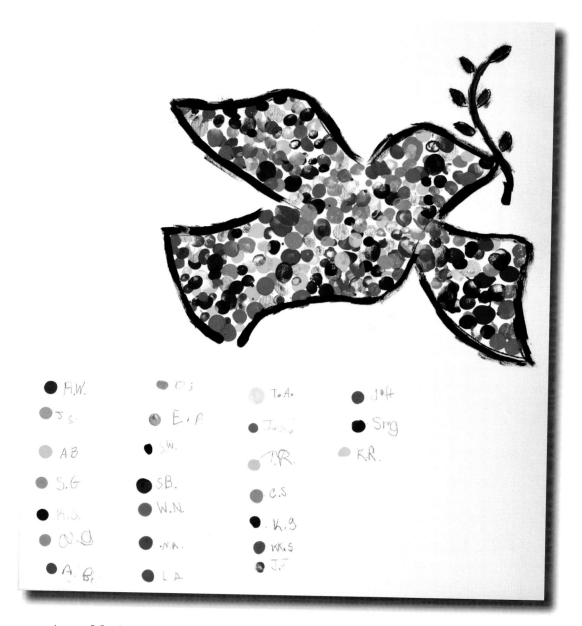

A collaboration by children from the Austin community

THE HOME
OF CHICAGO
WHITE SOX
SOX
SOUTHSIDE
HITMAN
Kevin Ellis

The Best

MALden
arms

FamilyCircle

LOVE

GeeK
GeeK
RULES

OTHER DAY
PARADISE

WORLD

Harold Washington Apts
Resident Services
4946 N Sheridan
Chicago, IL 60640

8 2

ARTIST INDEX

POSTCARD ARTISTS

Philip Austin
Mimi Avery
Barb
Elise Barber
Rosa Barton
Candace S. Beverly
Jimmy Brown
Phillip Carter
Children of Austin and Pullman Communities
Renee Cureton
Lawrence Davis
Sheila Davis
Clifford Dishmon
Chantee Evans
Fassination
Debra Grace
Herman Green
Irene Harris
Marcel Harris
Lasheena Jackson
Fredrick Johnson
Gregory Jones
Michael Korzun
Debra Little
Cynthia McCally
Michelle McKnuckles
Ollie Mason
M.E.P. (Anonymous)
N.R. Montague
Annie Peters
Arletha Plair
Clyde E. Rockward
Odessa Ross
T. Satyrs
Shiesha Smith
Diane Styles
Brenda C. Twine
Alma Watson
Arlene Young
And Others…